THE ART OF
CUTTING & FITTING

A Practical Manual

by

J. KING WILSON

of Messrs. John Morgan & Company,
15, Sackville Street, London, W.1

Winner of The Tailor & Cutter Gold Trophy 1950 and 1953.

THIRD EDITION

LONDON:
THE TAILOR AND CUTTER LIMITED
42-43 GERRARD STREET,
W.1.

First published 1948
Second Edition 1950
Third Edition 1958

CONTENTS

FOREWORD

By A. A. WHIFE, Technical Editor, The Tailor and Cutter;
Principal, The Tailor and Cutter Academy

THE fact that this book is being published in a third edition may be taken as an indication of its usefulness to the trade and of its value to those engaged in the practical side of it. In his preface to the first edition (1948) the late Theo. R. Hewitt, at that time secretary of the National Federation of Merchant Tailors, wrote:

" Mr. Wilson states that his primary object in producing this book was to help those cutters who have of necessity laid their shears aside for a number of years. He has done more than that: he has produced an invaluable book for *every* young cutter who, ' having equipped himself with sufficient knowledge to be able to produce a pattern by the method known as a system of cutting ', is now faced with the practical problem of developing that knowledge in the cutting and fitting rooms of an employer."

No better statement of the purpose and scope of *The Art of Cutting and Fitting* could have been made. Responsible as I am for the publication of the present edition, I can endorse Mr. Hewitt's words. The cutters he mentioned as having of necessity " laid their shears aside " were those who were on active service during the 1939–45 War. On their return to trade life they were in need of some kind of " refresher ". Mr. Wilson's book provided it.

However, it is not only an absence from the trade that can cause a certain amount of technical "rustiness". Experienced cutters know well enough that a complete familiarity with the procedures of cutting and fitting can cause a dulling of perception. Problems present themselves and the mind is not just ready to effect their solution. A book of this kind provides, in a straightforward and convenient form, a stimulus to thought and a " brushing away of cobwebs."

To the young and comparatively inexperienced cutter these pages must be of the greatest help. Whatever particular method of cutting and fitting he may have been taught, however he may be applying his knowledge of both, the principles contained in the author's explanations will be found applicable.

Mr. Wilson's style of writing may suggest a rather light-hearted approach to the subject; but this is not the case. He is only too well aware of the difficulties in the bespoke cutter's vocation; and he would be the last to assert that mastery of the contents of his book will eliminate every one of them. What he does set out to do is to provide all cutters—young and old—with the fruits of his own long and varied experience as a tailor and cutter and to give a reliable guide to the technique of cutting and the art of fitting.

INTRODUCTION

FIRST let me say that I am grateful to *The Tailor and Cutter* for publishing this third edition, not only for the personal satisfaction it gives me of doing something for my fellow craftsmen, but also because the method outlined has passed the test of criticism and has been proved in constant practice. I hope that it will be of great help to the newer generation of cutters and fitters.

My original purpose in writing *The Art of Cutting and Fitting*, first published in 1948, was to provide a "refresher course" for those whose cutters' careers' had been interrupted by the war. I realised from my own experience after the First World War that such a manual was sorely needed.

From the many letters from all over the world, and from frequent oral expressions of gratitude, I know that the book has been found helpful. Hence this third edition, for the benefit not only of old soldiers but of young members of our craft who may be struggling, possibly without help, with the intricacies of the science and art of cutting and fitting.

As far as I am aware, the book has been criticised only on the score that I have made the subject appear too easy. That, indeed, was my intention, so as to encourage and not to discourage the student. However, the latter should remember that a craft when mastered can be lucidly explained, but the acquisition of that craft may be a long and arduous process.

I

It is true to say, however, that the pursuit of excellence can be made considerably less arduous by the exercise of care in the main activities of garment cutting and fitting. What are those activities? There are, I think, three: Correct Measuring and Figure Observation; Careful Cutting; Accurate Fitting.

In the first I have combined what are really two things, but they are so closely related that they should always be regarded as one. Obviously, measures must be correctly taken if they are to be reliable as guides to cutting. Note must be taken of the characteristics of the figure, so that a picture of shape is obtained as well as an assessment of size.

When the measures and observations are recorded and are used in the cutting room, adaptations of the pattern (if a block is used) must be carefully made in accordance with them. This may seem too self-evident to deserve special comment; but it is surprising how often, in very busy cutting rooms where quite a lot of " rush " work is carried out, details are not taken into sufficient account. The result is greater trouble in the fitting room.

The fitting itself should be conducted in such a way as will achieve accuracy of actual fit, pleasing style lines and the satisfaction of the customer. The latter should be made to feel confident that the fitter knows what he is about and that he is endeavouring to interpret the customer's wishes—at the same time acting as a sartorial guide to him.

In the following pages I give methods of procedure which I have adopted in my own career and have found to be reliable. I have tried to indicate an ordered way of going to work—one which will give a reasonably clear picture of what has to be done by the efficient cutter and fitter.

CHAPTER I

TO BECOME A CUTTER AND FITTER

I ASSUME that that is your ambition. So I am going to talk to you about the art of cutting and fitting (as distinct from the science of producing a paper pattern). My observations are primarily intended for the young tailor who, by means of a tutor, a course of instruction at the Tailor and Cutter Academy, or the conscientious study of the various standard works on cutting, has equipped himself with sufficient knowledge to be able to produce a pattern by the method known as a system of cutting.

You, as an aspirant to cutting fame, have actually four different jobs to learn, and you will do well to regard them as four separate branches of your trade. It is the combined knowledge of all of them which produces the complete craftsman. The four matters to which I am referring are:—

(1) Making a garment.
(2) Cutting paper patterns.
(3) The art of cutting.
(4) The art of fitting.

I must say a few introductory words about each.

(1) SEWING

I imagine that you have already learned to sew and to make a garment to the satisfaction of your employer. If you haven't, don't you think you are putting the cart before the horse in tackling this book? Be that as it may, pride of craftsmanship and an infinite capacity for taking pains are the chief ingredients for success in this department.

(2) PAPER PATTERNS

Again, I expect (indeed I hope) that you are thoroughly proficient at producing paper patterns by the scientific method of cutting. This is comparatively simple, and can be accomplished with care and practice in a reasonably short time by anyone of ordinary intelligence—whether or not he be a practical tailor. There are various methods of producing a pattern for a given set of measures. Some are simple and some are complicated, but in the main they achieve the same result—namely, that of fitting what is generally known as a " normal " figure.

It is sometimes claimed on behalf of the more compli- cated scientific systems that they are capable of producing patterns to fit any figure. Most of these systems are based on direct measures, which are difficult enough to take and still more difficult to apply, so that the majority of bespoke cutters of experience use only the scientific method for the purpose of producing a normal, or standard, pattern, and then rely upon the art of cutting for their eventual success.

(3) THE ART OF CUTTING

Here success can be achieved only by careful measuring and careful observation of the figure, which together assist in balancing the various parts of the pattern. Of this I shall have quite a bit more to say later.

(4) THE ART OF FITTING

This is generally regarded as the most difficult of the four branches of your trade. *I cannot emphasize too strongly that there is no royal road to success in the art of fitting.* It is difficult to teach, and the art is acquired only after travelling the bitter (and often expensive) road of experience.

Don't be downhearted, however. I am going to save you from many heart-burnings and disappointments by pointing out to you in advance many of the snags that you will meet, and also make you familiar with a number of points that you would not discover for yourself in years of trial and error. I am merely warning you against undue optimism. We shall see that certain guiding principles can be laid down which will prove of incalculable assistance to you in overcoming the many difficulties you will encounter when you come to apply your theoretical or scientific knowledge to the more difficult and practical task of fitting.

In this small book, then, I propose to deal only with items (3) and (4) above, and I shall assume that you are already experienced in items (1) and (2).

CHAPTER II

MEASURING: HAVE YOU GOT IT TAPED?

WELL, have you? We have already noted that careful measuring of the figure is essential to success in connection with the art of cutting. No doubt you have already received not a little instruction on how to measure your customer, but a word or two on this much-neglected practice will not come amiss, because unless you are able to measure correctly, you will find that the pattern (however carefully prepared) will bear little or no resemblance to the size or shape of the figure.

Although measuring is a comparatively simple job, do not run away with the idea that proficiency can be attained without considerable *practice*. So *practise* on your friends and colleagues.

Take the first measures (that is, length of coat, width of back and sleeve length) *with the coat on*. This will serve as a guide to the length of coat that is suitable, and it will also indicate the utmost width of back the figure can carry. Remember, a side view of the figure gives a much clearer idea of its shape than a front or back view.

Remove the coat before you begin taking the remaining measures. You will probably find that your customer's *actual* figure is quite different from the one you have just seen with your own eyes. "A man owes much to his tailor", is a saying that cannot be denied (sometimes in more ways than one).

I have found it a very good plan to place an elastic belt round the waist of the customer. This gives a definite location of the waist; measures can then be taken from the belt upwards, at both front and back. If such a belt is not available, a length of plain white tape will serve quite well.

Take the chest measure on the easy side, and be sure that you keep your tape *well up at the back to cover the blades.* This precaution is most necessary, because if you allow the tape to slip down below the prominent part of the back (a not uncommon fault in the tyro), the measure will be *too small by one or two inches,* and so, of course, fatal to the production of your pattern. The novice is particularly liable to go wrong in this regard when the blades are carried high on the figure. Remember that in many systems of cutting it is on the size of your chest measurement that the size of your shoulder depends.

I cannot lay too much stress on this point. If you are not convinced, prove the point for yourself by placing the tape around your colleague's chest, first below the blades and then again with the tape over the blades. You will, I think, be amazed at the difference in the two measurements.

The waist-measure should be taken a little closer than that of the chest.

When taking the lower measures don't neglect the hip-measure (between the waist and the seat). For some reason that is quite inexplicable, this measure is frequently omitted in practice, with the most disastrous results to the trousers. When you bear in mind the fact that the figure often measures considerably more in this part of the anatomy than either the waist or the seat (particularly with those who have a tendency to corpulence) you will appreciate my point. If you neglect to take this measure you will meet with disaster: you will find that whilst the waist fly-button will button up easily enough, the services of a button-hook at least will have to be enlisted in order to get the trousers to meet below.

Thus the taking of measures is closely allied to the art of cutting, not only from the point of view of obtaining an accurate record of your customer's size and shape (an important but simple enough matter), but also because the process affords you an excellent opportunity of *studying the figure* for which you are about to cut. Your recorded measures should help to paint the picture for you, and your ability to take measures correctly will, in no small degree, be the measure of your success.

CHAPTER III

KEEPING YOUR BALANCE

My dictionary gives a number of different definitions of the word " balance ". The particular one upon which I want you to concentrate at the moment is " harmony of design and proportion ".

Having taken your measures and noted down in the measure-book your observations as to how your customer's figure differs from normal having regard to his chest measurement, your next consideration must be the preparation of a pattern.

BALANCE *is the corner-stone on which the successful production of your pattern depends*, and I want to talk to you about four different *kinds* of balances. These are:—

(1) Major Vertical Balance.
(2) Major Lateral Balance.
(3) Minor Vertical Balances.
(4) Minor Lateral Balances.

Perhaps these four new terms that I have invented will help to give you a fresh approach to that all-important factor in cutting, the production of a well-balanced pattern.

Now, I am well aware that honesty is the best policy, and also that it pays to go *straight* (so long as other people do so, too). I also know (if you share the experience of most West End tailors) that you will come across *crooks* in abundance in the ordinary course of business. But as we

9

turn our attention to the art of cutting, for goodness sake let us drop (and try to rule out for ever afterwards) those misleading, but all-too-common, references to " straight " and " crooked " shoulders and similar descriptions of the seat angle. These terms are misnomers and, as such, best forgotten. Let us, then, get back to the four balances.

1. *Major Vertical Balance.* By this I mean the relation your back section bears to your front section. It is the basis on which your garment depends for correct hang.

2. *Major Lateral Balance.* This balance describes the relation the neck-point of your forepart bears to the neck-point of your back. It is the basis on which the forward or backward movements of your forepart depend.

3. *Minor Vertical Balances.* These are the *small* adjustments that become necessary if you are going to follow the *vertical* shape of the figure (that is to say, a long or a short neck and square or sloping shoulders). These balances form the basis on which your minor vertical fitting depends. This takes in the length of the jacket (or coat) and the length of the sleeve.

4. *Minor Lateral Balances.* Here I am referring to the adjustments necessary in order to follow, first, the lateral shape of the figure, and secondly, the size (assisted by the measurements you have taken). These balances are the bases on which your *lateral* shape and also the size of the garment depend.

In the art of cutting, these four factors, or " balances ", as I have called them, should *all be treated separately.* The omission to consider any single one may not prove fatal, but together they result in the creation of a perfect pattern. You want to attain success in your trade? Very well, then. Look after the *balance* of your pattern, and your bank balance will look after itself.

The whole essence of the art of cutting consists of nothing more or less than the proper adjustment of your

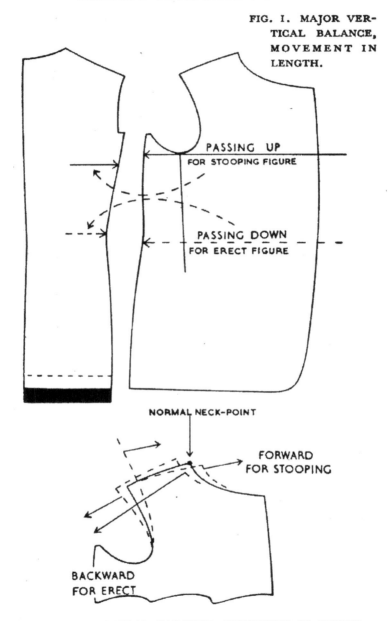

FIG. I. MAJOR VERTICAL BALANCE, MOVEMENT IN LENGTH.

PASSING UP
FOR STOOPING FIGURE

PASSING DOWN
FOR ERECT FIGURE

NORMAL NECK-POINT

FORWARD
FOR STOOPING

BACKWARD
FOR ERECT

FIG. 2. MAJOR LATERAL BALANCE, MOVEMENT IN WIDTH.

balances (both major and minor), which you will make from your *observation* of the customer's figure, as well as from the measures you have taken, using the block or standard pattern as a basis.

Simple direct measures will help you to find the shape of the figure for the minor balances. For example, with

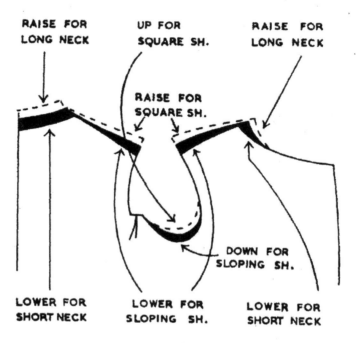

RAISE FOR LONG NECK   UP FOR SQUARE SH.   RAISE FOR LONG NECK

RAISE FOR SQUARE SH.

DOWN FOR SLOPING SH.

LOWER FOR SHORT NECK   LOWER FOR SLOPING SH.   LOWER FOR SHORT NECK

FIG. 3. MINOR VERTICAL BALANCES CONCERN SHAPE.

your tape depending from the collar-seam at the centre of the back, run your finger across the back horizontally from the shoulder-point to the tape. This will indicate to you the height of the collar-seam above the shoulder-point, which will usually be about 1¼ inches for a square shoulder, 2 inches for a normal shoulder and 2½ inches for sloping shoulders.

Jot down a note if you consider that a longer or shorter

back balance is needed. Consider the height of the blades. If they are pronounced, remember that some are carried high and others low. The high ones will need

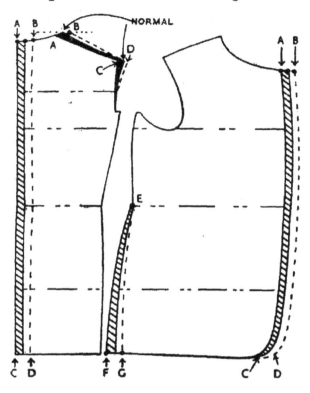

A - C = BIG BACK WITH SMALL FRONT
B - D = SMALL BACK WITH LARGE FRONT
E - F = LARGE HIPS. E G: FLAT HIPS

FIG. 4. MINOR LATERAL BALANCES CONCERN SHAPE AND SIZE.

the extra width at, say, 5 inches down; the low ones may require it as low as 9 inches down.

Observations such as " $\frac{1}{4}$ inch long back " or " $\frac{1}{4}$ inch short back " are useful. In fact, any disparity or divergence from the normal which cannot be measured should be noted with its estimated amount, as it will help you in painting the picture later on.

The accompanying diagrams are not drawn exactly to scale, and are not intended to show the correct adjustment for any specific case. They are merely illustrations of the *principles* you must apply in order to obtain well-balanced adjustments. Once you have mastered this new idea of balances, I venture to think that as a cutter it is unlikely that you will be found wanting.

CHAPTER IV

CULTIVATE AN EYE FOR FIGURES

IN the preceding chapter I tried to emphasise the importance of thinking afresh in terms of balances. Probably before we have finished dealing with the art of cutting and fitting you'll be a bit sick of them. I hope not, but nevertheless we shall have to consider them a lot more as we proceed. At the moment we are going to apply these friends of ours to the preparation of the pattern, using the same sequence as we have already laid down. Thus, we have:—

(1) THE MAJOR VERTICAL BALANCE

Take a look at Fig. 1. You will notice that the major vertical balance is arrived at by what is known as "passing up " the back or " passing down " the forepart. What is the object of this process? It is to arrange two pieces of cloth in such a way that they are perfectly balanced in their *vertical* relation for any given figure, bearing in mind that a variation from normal may be caused by its stoop or its erectness.

In most cases it is sufficient to pass a back up or down something between ¼ and 1 inch. In abnormal cases as much as 1 to 2 inches may be required. Now, don't imagine that there can be complete and final certainty in arriving at the correct amount to be passed up or down *at this stage.* The fixing of the amount cannot be finally determined until we come to the art of fitting in a later chapter. However, in preparing the pattern your aim must be to

get as near as possible to your ultimate goal. Success or
failure will be determined by the accuracy with which
you have taken your measurements and the care with
which you have taken *observation of your customer's figure.*

The major vertical balance is perhaps the most important of the four. It is certainly the most difficult to find
exactly in preparing the pattern. Emphatically, its maladjustment will cause greater trouble and add more to
your fitting-room difficulties than will a discrepancy in
any of the other balances. You will therefore pay attention to it accordingly.

Having made up your mind as to the amount of major
vertical balance you require, adjust your side-seam to give
effect to your decision. *Then dismiss this balance from your
mind* entirely, and turn your single-minded attention to
the next balance in the sequence. In other words, keep
each balance in a water-tight compartment.

(2) THE MAJOR LATERAL BALANCE

This balance is next in importance, and it will help you
to fix the correct position of the neck-point. Its function
is to move the forepart either forwards or backwards on a
lateral line, just as the maor vertical balance concerned
movement up or down on a *vertical* line. Consider Fig. 2
for a moment.

The adjustment of the major lateral balance consists
simply of a fore-and-aft movement. You will find this
process considerably easier than its predecessor. Further,
if you have diagnosed the major *vertical* balance correctly,
you will find that you have a definite pointer towards the
requirements for a proper *lateral* balance, because *the neck-
point goes forward with a stoop* (or long back balance) and
backward with an erect figure (or short back balance).   In
other words, *less* room is needed between the neck-point

and the front edge in a flat chest, and *more* room is needed in that vicinity for a full chest. So you see that a lateral movement of the neck-point takes material away from the front edge in the case of a flat chest, and adds to it in the case of a full chest. Just one last point. The amount the back has been passed up or down respectively is quite a useful guide by which to assess the amount of fore or aft movement required. Having decided on and given effect to your major lateral balance, you should dismiss it from your mind, and turn your whole attention to the next in our series of balances.

(3) The Minor Vertical Balances

See Fig. 3. Fixing these balances consists simply of making the slight local adjustments necessary in order to follow the *vertical shape* of the figure. There are four of these adjustments to be considered; they are:—

(i) Raising the back neck and gorge for a long neck.

(ii) Lowering the back neck and gorge for a short neck.

(iii) Raising the back and forepart shoulder-points in order to meet the requirements of a square shoulder.

(iv) Lowering them for a sloping shoulder, and at the same time raising or lowering the armhole a like amount.

All the above are quite elementary, but nevertheless highly important, adjustments. The amount required for each can only be arrived at in one way—that is, by means of your *observation of the figure*, together with the direct measurements you have taken. Have you noticed, by the way, that I continue to emphasize this matter of observation whilst the customer is being measured? It is vital to remember it.

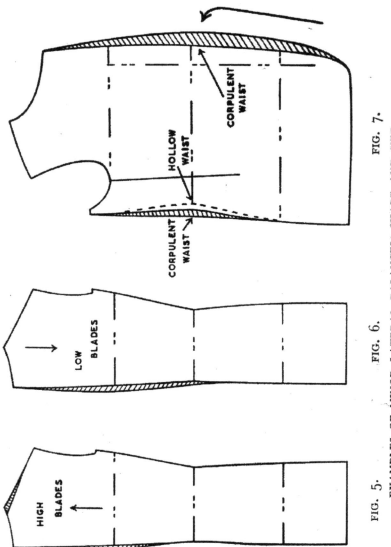

CORPULENT WAIST

HOLLOW WAIST

CORPULENT WAIST

FIG. 7.

LOW BLADES

FIG. 6.

HIGH BLADES

FIG. 5.   EXAMPLES OF MINOR LATERAL BALANCES: SHAPE AND SIZE.

Accuracy is essential to get the perfect shoulder. At the same time it is only fair to tell you that a *slight* maladjustment will not land you in the same trouble and disaster as would a correspondingly small error in the case of the major balances. The reason for this is, of course, that the minor vertical balances are adjustments of a *local* nature, and hence are more easily rectified.

Again, try to forget your jugglings with the previous balances as you proceed to tackle the final group.

(4) THE MINOR LATERAL BALANCES

These balances bear relation to both the *shape* and the *size* of the figure. They are more numerous than those in the previous groups because they deal with both these aspects. I want you to refer to Figs. 4, 5, 6 and 7 as we proceed.

First, look at Fig. 4. You will notice that it deals with a big back with a small front, or with the reverse— in other words, a flat or prominent chest. When your measures and observations indicate that you are dealing with a big back, your chest-measure (when applied to the pattern) will *automatically reduce* the size of your front. Similarly, if a small back is called for, your applied chest-measure will *automatically increase* the size of your front. You will apply similar adjustments to a flat waist and hips or to a prominent waist and hips, as the case may be.

Next turn to Figs. 5 and 6. In spite of their simplicity, you will readily see that a round back, prominent blades, high blades or low blades all call for minor local adjustments in a *lateral* direction in order to conform to the shape of the figure.

Lastly let us look at Fig. 7. Having made the above adjustments with an eye to shape, you should now measure up your pattern for *size* at the chest, waist and hips.

Your pattern is now complete, with the exception of the sleeve, the head of which should be adjusted to conform to the height of the shoulders. If you have to contend with square shoulders, what adjustment will you make? Why, of course, you will *slightly raise* the head of the sleeve. And for sloping shoulders? Slightly lower the head. You are beginning to get the idea, I think. If you have not quite grasped it yet, it might be as well for you to re-read this chapter before going on ahead.

By the way, I ought perhaps to tell you why I insisted on your forgetting each adjustment as you turned to the next balance in the sequence—that is, keeping each group of balances in its own separate compartment. The object is twofold. First, in this way you make each set of balances do its own work without trespassing upon another. Secondly, the separate consideration of the different balances will materially assist you in your *diagnosis* when you come to the matter of fitting. You will find that this method simplifies the issue and helps to keep your mind unconfused.

This chapter has been rather heavy going, hasn't it? But the effort has been well worth while, and I have no doubt you have learnt quite a bit. Let me end on a personal note. During the war (when labour was at a premium), having used for over thirty years the old rule-of-thumb method, I was forced to find a means by which *alterations could be cut down to the irreducible minimum.* This, mark you, in an exacting West End business. After a good deal of cogitation, I found what I sought in the group-balance system. I soon discovered that it reduced the margin of error in two ways: first, in preparing the pattern (where no balance, major or minor, can possibly escape your notice), and later, as we shall see when we come to consider it, in the art of fitting. With fitting, the cause of every effect needs to be sought for. When one has traced the cause it is a comparatively simple matter to apply the appropriate cure.

Let me explain this with an example. When using the old-fashioned method of, say, crooking or straightening a shoulder, you were told (respectively) to lengthen or shorten the front shoulder, in doing which you were rolling two, or even three, sets of balances into one. By my modern method the lengthening or shortening of the front balance has already been done for you, by passing the back down for an erect figure, or up for a stooping figure. So you can see that the neck-point is used for *one* purpose only—namely, in connection with the fore or aft movement of the front. If necessary, the neck-point will be lowered or raised *automatically* when you come to the minor vertical balances.

Now, by keeping each group of balances in their watertight compartments, you systematically provide for every possible contingency. Nothing is missed. Nothing *can* be missed. I don't think I am going too far in comparing the old-fashioned rule-of-thumb method to a cross-word puzzle, in which a given clue permits various alternative answers. If we continue the analogy, the new method might be compared to a jig-saw puzzle, which provides for one solution and one only. Each piece must fit into its appointed place, and no other. Your success is directly dependent on your ability to *observe size and shape*. I don't want you to think that your immediate diagnosis will always be correct—but at least you will have a definite method to apply.

Postscript.—You will, of course, apply the same principles to the waistcoat as you have already done to the coat pattern.

CHAPTER V

LET'S LOOK AT SOME LEGS

I AM referring to legs inside their trousers and, as you may have guessed, we shall again apply our old friends the balances to this problem.

Similar principles of balance to those we have already considered apply to your trouser-block (if you use one) or in the drafting of your pattern, *but with one marked difference.* You will readily appreciate that there can be *no major vertical* balance in the trousers (which hang from hips or braces) in the sense that there is in the coat (which rests upon the shoulders). Obviously it would be quite stupid for me to tell you to pass up the back of a pair of trousers, because all you would succeed in doing would be to give a little more length in the vicinity of the back brace-buttons. This can easily be done if necessary, as we shall see when we come to our minor vertical balances. Similarly, if one leg-seam or side-seam were to be passed up or down independently of the other, nothing more than a twist in the trousers would result. If it is occasionally found necessary to apply the latter adjustment, this is solely due to the fact that the trousers have been badly put together; that is to say, the balance-marks on the leg-seam or side-seam have been allowed to go adrift.

There is, however, a definite major vertical balance controlled by the seat-seam. But, as the same seam controls our major *lateral* balance, we consider them as one, and this is what happens. (See Fig. 8.) According to the roundness or flatness of the seat, the hind part of the trousers requires longer or shorter balance, respectively. You can effect this balance by giving a shorter seat-angle for the flat seat, or a longer seat-angle for the round seat.

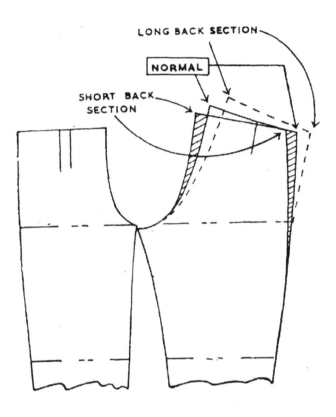

FIG. 8. MAJOR VERTICAL BALANCE, MOVEMENT IN LENGTH.

This you do by bringing the seat-seam on the waist-line *inwards* (or nearer to the fork) for a flat seat, or by carrying it *outwards* (or away from the fork) for a round seat. Thus, in effect, you are either shortening or lengthening the back of the trousers in relation to the front.

The Major Lateral Balance

Before reading on, take a look at Fig. 9. In applying
the major lateral balance, the seat-seam *as a whole* (as

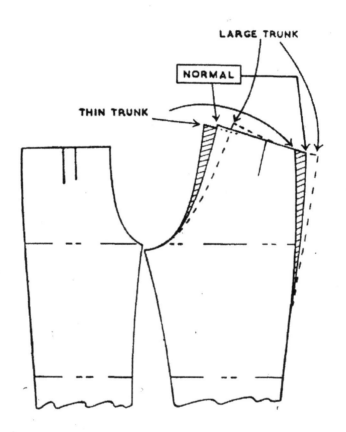

FIG. 9.   MAJOR LATERAL BALANCE, MOVEMENT IN WIDTH.

distinct from the seat-angle) is placed farther in or out. In
other words, it is carried towards the fork for a thin trunk,
and is carried farther out, or back (away from the fork),
for a large trunk, *regardless of the vertical balance.* Re-

member, the seat-seam plays the same rôle in trouser-cutting as the neck-point does in coat-cutting. By its lateral movement it transfers cloth from one place to another.

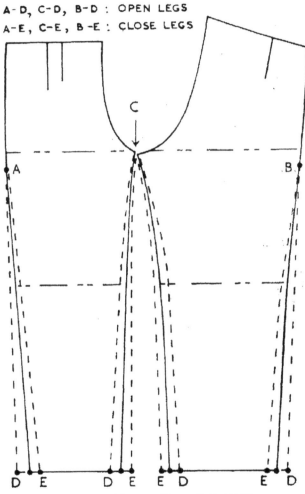

A-D, C-D, B-D : OPEN LEGS
A-E, C-E, B-E : CLOSE LEGS

FIG. 10. MAJOR LATERAL BALANCE.

Now look at Fig. 10, which deals with *openness and closeness of the legs*. We consider this matter as one of major lateral balance, because the openness and close-

C

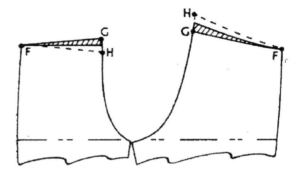

F-G: LONG FRONT WITH SHORT BACK
F-H: SHORT FRONT WITH LONG BACK

FIG. 11.   EXAMPLE OF MINOR VERTICAL BALANCES
(CONCERNS SHAPE AND LENGTH).

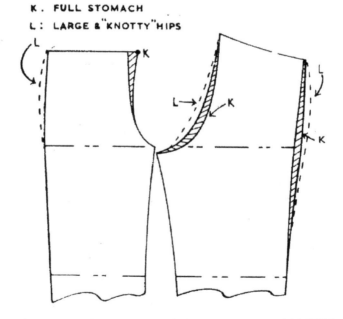

K. FULL STOMACH
L: LARGE & "KNOTTY" HIPS

FIG. 12.   EXAMPLE OF MINOR LATERAL BALANCES
(CONCERNS SHAPE AND SIZE).

ness of the legs are dependent on *balance* rather than on size. It is obvious what happens. The openness or closeness of the leg-seam will simply be regulated by the openness or closeness of the legs of your customer's figure.

THE MINOR VERTICAL BALANCES

Have a glance at Fig. 11. You will find these balances quite simple if you bear in mind that height is given to the back, in the vicinity of the back brace-buttons, if the figure bends forward, and that more length is required in the front if your customer is blessed with the(proverbial) proportions of an alderman.

THE MINOR LATERAL BALANCES

See Fig. 12. These relate to matters of shape and size, and in order to obtain them correctly, you will apply the waist-, hip- and seat-measures. You will be guided both by your measures and by your *observation* of the figure, with a view to deciding where material is required to follow the shape and where it is not. For example, extra material is needed on the *front* for a full stomach and on the *side* in order to cope with large and knotty hips. You have already fixed the position of your seat-angle, which should be left *untouched*.

In general, when preparing the pattern for your trousers it is wise to keep the seat-line well open (that is to say, well back from the fork). If you do this you give the trousers a chance of breathing. When you have finished, hold them up by the top of the side-seams just as if you were about to put them on, and then look down into them and see what trunk-room you have between the fork-line and the seat. There must be sufficient room for the trunk to drop into them. Otherwise there will be trouble in the region of the fork and seat-seam. A seat-line that is too close will irritate your customer—literally.

CHAPTER VI

FOR THOSE WHO SUFFER FROM BAD FITS

In this chapter I want to tell you, not how to cure bad fits (as suggested by my title), but rather how to *avoid* them. From which you will gather that we are going to consider the gentle art of fitting. The subject is the most interesting, and at the same time the most difficult, of all. It presents a large field for thought and study, and it is only when we get to this stage that we *realize how many mistakes we have made* in measuring, in observation of the figure and in preparing the pattern.

I cannot emphasize too strongly that there is only *one way* to learn the art, and that is by constant practice. There is no short cut to proficiency. As in most walks of life, experience is the best (albeit the most expensive) instructor. You simply cannot acquire the art by reading instructions out of a book, no matter how brilliant the author and no matter how apt a pupil you are. So my first counsel to you is: if you want to learn cutting and fitting, *start* on cutting and fitting, and *keep going.*

I am not forgetting, of course, that the object of this little book is to guide your feet into the right path and to point out in advance the traps and stumbling-blocks that await the uninitiated. But you'll never get anywhere unless you start walking.

I have gone to some pains to find the most interesting and, at the same time, the most complete and efficient method of presenting the subject, with an eye to assisting you as to the lines upon which to think. I have been unable to discover a better method than what I may call an " IMMEDIATE ACTION " system, like that taught to the recruit by the Army Instructional Staff for remedying stoppages and faults in an automatic weapon.

Most of you will have served in one of the Services, and know (only too well!) the sort of method I have in mind.

When, in the P.B.I. (or elsewhere), you learned a new weapon, you were taught holding and aiming, elementary handling, and so forth. Preparing the pattern corresponds to these. Eventually you were trained in stoppages and I.A. For the benefit of the uninitiated, I had better explain that I.A. (or Immediate Action) is the action that the firer of an automatic weapon takes immediately it ceases to fire. The purpose of I.A. is twofold: first, to diagnose the fault (that is, the reason why the gun has ceased to fire) as quickly as possible, and, secondly, to remedy the defect without delay. Eventually, after endless practice, the recruit will know his I.A. so well that his reaction to any stoppage is *instinctive*.

Perhaps you begin to perceive why I am modelling my method on that of the Army. I am going to give you various types of I.A., as applied to the procedure of fitting, so that in time you will *instinctively react* to " mechanical " faults that have arisen in preparing the pattern. Every possible contingency will be systematically provided for by a " school solution ", which will demonstrate the cause of every effect and, of course, give you the remedy.

It is a far cry from a Tommy-gun to the fitting-room (although even in those serene surroundings the need for such a weapon may occasionally be felt), and I can imagine that if by mischance this book should find its way into the hands of a cutter who has arrived, he would weep tears of blood at the very idea of his art being so debased. But that, I regret, neither alarms nor deters me.

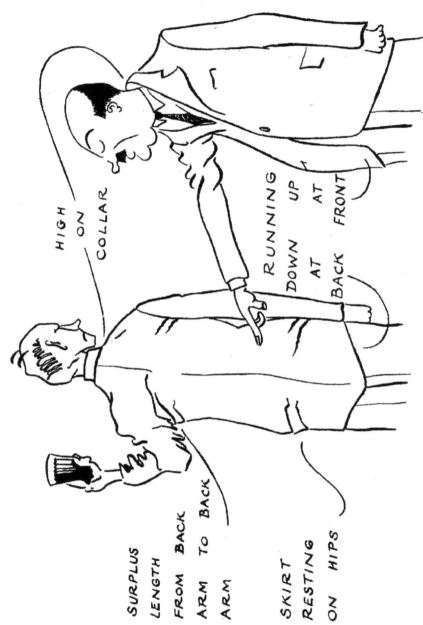

HIGH ON COLLAR

RUNNING UP AT FRONT

RUNNING DOWN AT BACK

SURPLUS LENGTH FROM BACK ARM TO BACK ARM

SKIRT RESTING ON HIPS

FIG. 13. MAJOR VERTICAL BALANCE TOO LONG.

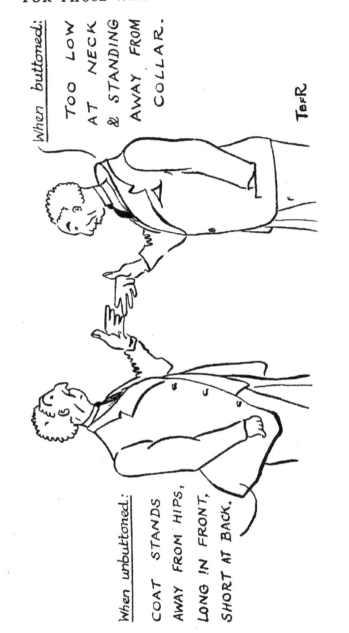

FIG. 14. MAJOR VERTICAL BALANCE TOO SHORT.

I am sorry to say that lack of *fundamental* training and, particularly, failure to apply a *reasoned* method of procedure in the fitting-room results in many young cutters, who would call themselves experienced, indulging in a great deal of disjointed and woolly thinking. Some, I fear, emerge with a harassed expression, from the fitting-room, scarcely knowing the seat of their trousers from the elbow of their coat, and subsequently applying the hit-or-miss method to the marking up. And the result? Unnecessary alterations, waste of time, waste of money. A bad business altogether. Hence my insistence on your learning the groundwork thoroughly.

You should aim at being so technically efficient that you not only observe every fault during the process of fitting (of course you'll do that), but that you also mentally note the appropriate remedy *at the same time*. Your job is to convey to the garments, by means of carefully made chalk-marks, the faults that you have observed and, hence, the remedies that you propose, so that the picture is clearly painted for you by the time you come to mark up the garment. I will go even farther. Your aim should be not only to make the alteration marks at the time of fitting with care and accuracy, but to make them so explicit and so *self-explanatory* that *any* intelligent tailor can, if necessary, proceed with the making up without further reference to you.

You will accomplish this and more if you will only practise assiduously the mental immediate action of the fitting-room that I am about to unfold. You will find it laborious at first, but it will pay a handsome dividend in the end. Apply the same sequences in fitting as you did in preparing the pattern. You will remember that these are:—

(1) Major Vertical Balance.
(2) Major Lateral Balance.
(3) Minor Vertical Balances.
(4) Minor Lateral Balances.

With which I think we cannot do better than bring this chapter to an end and make a fresh start.

CHAPTER VII.

CUT AND COME AGAIN

PERHAPS you think that is a curious title for a chapter on fitting? What I intend to imply is that I am about to give you a series of tables that contain the whole quintessence—pith, core, guts, sum and substance, or what you will—of the art of fitting. If you want to make a success of your career, you will *read, mark, learn and inwardly digest* this chapter, until the very pages become well-thumbed and dog-eared. If in the P.B.I. you were ever responsible for an automatic weapon, you were made to learn I.A. until you knew it backwards, because your life (and the lives of others) depended on your *automatic reaction* to a stoppage or fault. Need I rub the lesson in? Cut and come again.

By the way, take a look at Figs. 13 and 14.

By the use of the following tables fitting can be reduced almost to a simple mechanical process. The tables are (if you like) the mechanics of fitting. The art lies in the ability to discern immediately which one or more of the numerous balances are at fault, and also in not confusing one with another. If the diagnosis is wrong, the mechanical process of adjustment will obviously be wrong also. If you learn to follow the sequence of the tables as a drill, you will find that it will assist you in your diagnosis.

34

MAJOR VERTICAL BALANCE

Sequence	Effect	Cause	Immediate action
(1)	High on collar. Surplus cloth in length from back arm to back arm. Skirt resting on hips.	Major vertical balance too long.	Pass down the back. Guide for amount is the loose cloth you are able to pick up between the fingers across the back.
(2a)	Coat standing off or away from the hips when fronts are unfastened.	Vertical balance too short.	Pass up the back. As a guide for the amount, lift the coat off the shoulders, pulling it down at the back until the skirt rests easily on the hips. The amount the collar is low and stands away from neck is the adjustment necessary.
(2b)	Coat too low and standing away from neck when fronts are fastened. Lateral folds under arms.		

MAJOR LATERAL BALANCE

Sequence	Effect	Cause	Immediate action
(1)	Coat tight on top button. Running on at bottom of front edge. Surplus material in front of arm. Shoulder of coat resting on the arm. Vertical folds under arm.	Neck-point too far forward—i.e., too near the front edge.	Put neck-point farther back — i.e., away from front edge. A guide for the amount of adjustment is the amount the coat appears small at top button and surplus material in front of arm. Rarely more than $\frac{1}{2}$ in. to $\frac{3}{4}$ in. is called for.
(2)	Coat too big on top button. Running away at bottom of front edge. Poor in front of armhole.	Neck-point too far back—i.e., too far away from front edge.	Reverse the above procedure, amount depending on how much too big at top button.

MINOR VERTICAL BALANCES

Sequence	Effect	Cause	Immediate action
(1)	Collar too high or too low.	Neck too high or too low.	Raise or lower collar.
(2)	Coat standing off neck and resting too closely on shoulders. Crease under collar.	Shoulder not square enough, or more shoulder room necessary.	Square the shoulders by taking in neck or letting out shoulder point. If depth of armholes is correct, use the former. If too high, use the latter method.
(3)	Coat too loose or big at shoulders point.	Shoulder not sloping enough or too square.	Take in shoulder-point or let out neck-point. If armhole is correct, use the former; if too high, use the latter method.
(4)	Sleeve creases below forearm and hindarm.	Insufficient vertical balance or crown.	Give more crown to sleeve-head.
(5)	Sleeve creases across crown.	Too much vertical balance or crown.	Reduce crown of sleeve-head.

MINOR LATERAL BALANCES

Sequence	Effect	Cause	Immediate action
(1)	Tight crease under collar across back.	Back too small at top from shoulder-point to shoulder-point.	Let out top of back. Check neck-point to prevent neck of coat becoming too long.
(2)	Diagonal crease from blades towards side waist of back. Loose at back arm, with coat standing away at bottom of centre back seam.	Insufficient room across back at blade bones. Shape of back incorrect.	Let out back on centre seam at blades.

MINOR LATERAL BALANCES (*Continued*)

Sequence	Effect	Cause	Immediate action
(3)	Tight lateral creases under arms at chest and waist.	Too little room between side-seam and front of armhole, or coat too small.	Let out through side-seams.
(4)	Loose vertical folds under arm at chest and waist.	Too much width between side seam and armhole, or coat too big.	Take in through side-seams.
(5)	Tight diagonal crease from hip at side-seam towards front of armhole.	Insufficient hip room.	Let out side-seam over round of hip.
(6)	Coat too big on front edge.	Measures incorrectly taken or wrongly applied. If the latter, too big in front section to the detriment of back section.	Take new measures. Let out back section. Reduce front section.
(7)	Coat too small on front edge.	Reverse of above.	Reverse above procedure.

In order to amplify the tables, let us run through the sequence again. We shall begin to see how errors crept in whilst we were preparing the pattern, and, at the same time, learn how to prevent confusion in making the necessary adjustments. Keep a finger in the appropriate page of the tables as we go over them together.

MAJOR VERTICAL BALANCE

Sequence (1). Surplus cloth in length from back arm to back arm, etc. The cause of this was failure to observe that the figure was more erect than normal. Don't confuse this symptom with that resulting in a tight

crease under the collar, as in Sequence (1) of the Minor
Lateral Balances.

Sequence (2a). Coat standing off, or away from, the hips.
This has resulted from failure to observe a stoop or a
thickness of the back of the figure. Don't confuse this
with Sequence (2) of the Minor Lateral Balances, in
which the coat stands away at the centre of the back.

Sequence (2b). Coat too low and standing away from neck.
There is a subtle difference between this effect and that
which I have described as "Coat standing off neck"
in Sequence (2) of the Minor Vertical Balances. If
you observe carefully you will learn to spot it every time.

MAJOR LATERAL BALANCE

Sequence (1). Coat tight on top button. Here the cause
was failure to observe that the figure was more than
normally full in the chest. Don't mix this up with
Sequence (7) of the Minor Lateral Balances—they are
somewhat similar at first glance. Again, the garment
may be too small generally.

Sequence (2). Coat too big on top button, etc. The cause
of this was a failure to notice that the customer's figure
stooped or was flatter on the chest than normal. You
must learn to distinguish this fault from that in Sequence
(6) of the Minor Lateral Balances.

MINOR VERTICAL BALANCES

Sequence (1). Collar too high or too low. This has
resulted from failure to observe that the neck was longer
or shorter than normal. The symptoms are not to be
confused with those in Sequences (1) and (2b) of the
Major Vertical Balance.

Sequence (2). Coat standing off neck and resting too closely
on shoulders. This has arisen because of a failure to
observe that the figure was squarer or larger in the

shoulders than in the normal case. Don't confuse this with Sequence (2b) of the Major Vertical Balance.

Sequence (3). Coat too loose or big at shoulder-point. The cause in this instance was failure to notice that the customer's figure was more sloping or smaller in the shoulders than normal. This must not be confused with the effect described as " loose at back arm " in Sequence (2) of the Minor Lateral Balances.

Sequences (4) *and* (5), as you can see for yourself, are a necessary consequence of (2) and (3) above.

Minor Lateral Balances

Sequence (1). Tight crease under collar across back. The cause of this was your failure to observe either that the back was big across the top from shoulder-point to shoulder-point, or that the blades were very high. Don't mix up this fault with that in Sequence (2) of the Minor Vertical Balances.

Sequence (2). Diagonal crease from blades towards side waist of back, etc. This has resulted from failure to observe either that the blade-bones were more prominent than usual, or that the centre of the back was rounder or longer than normal. You must distinguish this sequence from that which I described as " standing away from hips " under Sequence (2a) of the Major Vertical Balance. The two symptoms are, I know, very alike, and the inexperienced eye frequently makes the wrong diagnosis. So be warned.

Sequence (3). Tight lateral creases under arms at chest and waist. Here you failed to notice that the figure was larger than normal between the forearm and back arm. This is not to be confused with " lateral folds under arms " in Sequence (2b) of the Major Vertical Balance.

Sequence (4). Loose vertical folds under arm at chest and waist. These arose from your failure to note that the figure was smaller than usual between the forearm and the back arm. Don't confuse this with the vertical folds under the arm described in Sequence (1) of the Major Lateral Balance.

Sequence (5). Tight diagonal crease from hip at side-seam towards front armhole. This has come about because you didn't notice that either the hip or the seat was larger than normal. Compare this with " skirt resting on hips " in Sequence (1) of the Major Vertical Balance, and note the difference.

Sequences (6) *and* (7). Coat too big or too small on front edge. *Assuming that your measures were correct,* this is the result of failing to note *whereabouts* the size on the figure which varies from the normal was carried. This is quite different from Sequences (1) and (2) of the Major Lateral Balance.

The Waistcoat

For the waistcoat apply the same principle as you did for the coat. The Major Vertical Balance can be ½ inch to 1 inch longer, so as to prevent bulging at the neck when the wearer is sitting down.

CHAPTER VIII

POINTS ABOUT PANTS

FROM the very moment that I started thinking about trousers, an old rhyme has been running insistently through my head. So much so that I feel bound to quote it. Here it is:—

There was a little girl, who had a little curl
Right in the middle of her forehead.
When she was good, she was very very good,
But when she was bad, she was horrid.

" What on earth ", you may well ask, " has that to do with trousers?" And the answer, of course, is, " Nothing at all ". *Except* that the last line is so apposite to our subject that I could not refrain from mentioning it. When trousers are bad, they are very bad indeed and, further, in the hands of the inexperienced *they usually get progressively worse with each attempt to alter them.* From which you will gather (believe it or not!) that the art of fitting trousers is more difficult than that of fitting coats. The reason for this is that one seam (as I explained in connection with preparing the trouser pattern)—namely, the seat-seam—is used for *both* the Major Balances (Vertical and Lateral).

Having said that, we may proceed without delay to consideration of our leg drill, which, like that for coats, must be read, marked, learned and inwardly digested. For the effect of some faults have a look at Figs. 15 and 16.

MAJOR VERTICAL BALANCE

Sequence	Effect	Cause	Immediate action
(1)	Too much length on seat-seam. Surplus cloth in length under seat.	Seat-angle too long.	Shorten seat-angle by bringing seat-line inwards at waist — *i.e.*, towards fork.
(2)	Too short on seat-seam, causing pull and uncomfortable look under seat and length on side-seam.	Seat-angle too short.	Lengthen seat-angle by putting seat-line backwards at waist — *i.e.*, away from fork.

MAJOR LATERAL BALANCE

Sequence	Effect	Cause	Immediate action
(1)	Trousers too tight in fork, seat-seam disappearing between crevice in legs. Tight lateral creases under seat.	Insufficient trunk or fork room.	Place seat-line backwards—*i.e.*, away from fork—at seat and waist, letting out same amount at side-seam.
(2)	Trousers too full in fork. Loose vertical folds in seat.	Too much trunk or fork room.	Place seat-line inwards — *i.e.*, towards fork—taking in same amount at side-seam.
(3)	Lateral folds inside leg, destroying straight hang from fork to bottom of leg-seam.	Leg-seam too open, or placed too far back, or away from fork.	Place leg-seam inwards — *i.e.*, towards fork—taking same amount off side-seam.
(4)	Lateral folds on outside of leg, with apparent strain from fork to outside of foot.	Leg-seam too close or placed too far inwards in relation to fork.	Place leg-seam outwards—*i.e.*, away from fork—adding same amount to side-seam at knee and bottom.

MINOR VERTICAL BALANCES

Sequence	Effect	Cause	Immediate action
(1)	Tight crease from front brace-button towards fork.	Insufficient front rise.	Raise front at top of fly to nothing at side-seams. Allow more length to cover round of belly.
(2)	Loose lateral folds across front below waist.	Front rise too long.	Lower fronts at top of fly to nothing at side-seam. Rarely necessary except in case of very hollow waist.
(3)	Tight vertical crease from back brace-button towards fork.	Insufficient back rise.	Raise back rise to nothing at side-seams.
(4)	Loose lateral folds across back under waist.	Too much back rise.	Lower back rise at back brace-buttons to nothing at sides.

MINOR LATERAL BALANCES

Sequence	Effect	Cause	Immediate action
(1)	Tight lateral creases across belly.	Insufficient room at top of fly.	Let out front at prominent part of belly.
(2)	Loose vertical folds at belly, behind fly.	Too much lateral room across belly.	Take in at top of front.
(3)	Tight lateral creases across hips.	Insufficient lateral room over hips.	Let out side-seams at hips.
(4)	Loose vertical folds at hips.	Too much hip room.	Take in side-seams at hips.
(5)	Tight lateral creases across seat.	Insufficient seat room.	Let out side-seams at seat.
(6)	Loose vertical folds at seat.	Too much seat room.	Take in side-seams at seat.

Once again let us amplify the tables by running through the sequence, in the same way as we did with coats.

Major Vertical Balance

Sequence (1). Too much length on seat-seam, surplus cloth in length under seat. This has resulted from your

FIG. 15. MINOR VERTICAL BALANCE. INSUFFICIENT FRONT RISE.

failure when measuring to observe that the seat was flat and that the size of the seat-measure was to be found on the hips. Don't confuse this error in balance with that in Sequence (4) of the Minor Vertical Balances, where there is too much back rise.

Sequence (2). Too short on seat-seam, etc., causing pull on seat. The cause here was a failure when measuring to observe that the seat was prominent. Don't mix this up with Sequence (3) of the Minor Vertical Balances, which deals with insufficient back rise.

SEAT ANGLE   SEAT ANGLE
TOO LONG.   TOO SHORT.

FIG. 16. MAJOR VERTICAL BALANCE.

MAJOR LATERAL BALANCE

Sequence (1). Trousers too tight in fork, etc. How did this arise? Because when measuring you overlooked the fact that the figure was thick in depth and required more trunk room than usual. You must learn to distinguish this cause and effect from those in Sequence (2) of the Major Vertical Balance, where the seat-angle is too short.

Sequence (2). Trousers too full in fork, etc. What is the cause here? Simply your omission to note when measuring that your customer's figure had more width than thickness; in other words, that less trunk or fork room than usual was required. This symptom is not to be confused with that of Sequence (1) of the Major Vertical Balance, where, as we have seen, the seat-angle was too long.

Sequence (3). Lateral folds inside leg, etc. This has happened because you missed the fact that the figure stands with legs close together.

Sequence (4). Lateral folds on outside of leg, etc. What was the cause? Simply, failure to observe that the figure stood with legs apart.

Minor Vertical Balances

Sequence (1). Tight crease from front brace-button, etc. The reason for this effect is that when measuring you quite overlooked the fact that the belly was unusually prominent and required more length, as well as width, in its vicinity.

Sequence (2). Loose lateral folds, etc. This has come about because you failed to observe that the waist was exceptionally hollow.

Sequence (3). Tight vertical crease, from back to fork. What was the cause here? It was that you were not careful to observe that the figure stooped from the waist and, hence, that it required longer back rise. Don't confuse this with Sequence (2) of the Major Vertical Balance, which is caused by a too short seat-angle.

Sequence (4). Loose lateral folds under waist. These folds are caused by too much back rise: this means that you overlooked the fact that the figure was exceptionally hollow at the back waist. This symptom must not be confused with that in Sequence (1) of the Major Vertical Balance, in which, as we have seen, the seat-angle was too long.

Minor Lateral Balances

Sequence (1). Tight lateral creases across the belly: insufficient room at the top of the fly. This has been caused by your failure when measuring to observe that the belly was carried well forward. As a result, you didn't allow sufficient Minor Lateral Balance to meet this protuberance.

Sequence (2). Loose vertical folds at belly, etc. The cause of this was your failure to notice that excessive size in the measure below the waist was carried on the hips, and not on the belly. In other words, adjustment for the Minor Lateral Balance has been made in the wrong place.

Sequence (3). Tight lateral creases across hips. What has caused these? Here you failed to observe the excessive size of the hips, and so got your adjustment of the Minor Lateral Balance wrong.

Sequence (4). Loose vertical folds at hip, etc. These have arisen because you omitted to note that the figure had flat hips, and so your adjustment for Minor Lateral Balance was incorrect.

Sequence (5). Tight lateral crease at seat, etc. The cause of this was your omission to observe the prominence of the seat. Hence you did not provide sufficient room in making your adjustment for Lateral Balance.

Sequence (6). Loose vertical folds at seat, etc. This is the result of your overlooking the flatness of the customer's seat. Thus (in contrast to the mistake in Sequence (5)) in making the Minor Lateral adjustment you provided too much room.

CHAPTER IX

GOLDEN TIPS

You must not conclude from the title either that I've got something special for the 2.30 for you, or that I am going to recommend a new blend of tea. In this and the next chapter I am going to offer you a few tit-bits with which I hope to stimulate your sartorial appetite. Some of them are, I venture to think, worth their weight in gold.

I am frequently asked, " Why do you fellows need so many fittings? After all—I mean to say—the ready-made stores claim that they can cater for everybody out of their limitless supply of different shapes and sizes." That kind of remark is *partly* true, and, like all half-truths, dangerous. The real answer is that the salesman of the ready-made has only to find a figure to fit one of his numerous shapes and sizes, whereas the bespoke cutter has to make a suit to fit the size and shape of his customer's figure—and to fit his mind as well! A vastly different proposition.

It is true that the makers of ready-to-wear clothing have made rapid strides, particularly in America, during the years between the wars. The off-the-peg merchants, having enticed members of the bespoke trade with tempting wages, have picked their brains and, of course, benefited from the knowledge so gained.

I admit, too, that it is within the scope of any cutter of experience to produce patterns and to have garments made up for stock to fit quite a wide range of figures. A well-balanced coat will fit a range of figures having a similar chest measurement and, subject to slight adjustments in the Minor Vertical and Lateral Balances, many figures can be catered for thus. So, for example, a generous 40-inch chest-block will look reasonably well on a large-shouldered 38-inch figure: it would not look too badly on a small-shouldered 42-inch chest. But *we* are not concerned with the ready-to-wear business, but with our ability to make a suit to fit our customer's particular eccentricities of build satisfactorily.

Here, then, is tip number one. *In cutting your pattern, always err on the big side.* The only thing you cannot afford to have too large is the armhole, which, in the interest of the still-sought-after drape of to-day, should (so far as is consistent with comfort) be kept as small and as high up as possible. The armhole should resemble the shape of an egg, rather than the horseshoe of the old designs. It must, however, be large enough to take the sleeve comfortably.

A manufacturing tailor in a considerable way of business, for whom I have in the past made clothes for more years than I care to remember, invariably referred to me as the " safety-first " tailor. He used to say, " I wouldn't employ you in my factory—you waste too much cloth." To which I replied, " *I would rather waste cloth than waste time*, which is just what I should do if I started off with my suit on the small side."

My second tip is that *a big back will save you from many a big headache.* I could add that you will be saved from a number of *minor* ailments, too. Of your Major Vertical Balance, I would advise that you should keep it on the long side. And the reason? Simply this. It is easier to judge how much you require to shorten a back than to judge by how much it should be lengthened. In any case, the long back balance causes less trouble at the start.

Thirdly, err (if you must) to the extent of keeping your Major Lateral Balance (in other words, the *neck-point*) on the forward side—that is, *towards the front*. This gives the coat a better chance of a start in life, and will help you in the fitting of the shoulder.

Next, regarding your *Minor Vertical Balances, be generous rather than stinting*. Always keeping a watchful eye on the shape and depth of the armhole. Don't be stingy in dealing with your *Minor Lateral Balances* either. You will find that it is a far simpler matter to judge how much to take in at any given point than how much to let out.

Next, I advise you to *keep your sleeve as full as possible at the top*. A small sleeve is an abomination. Many an armhole has been mutilated in the interest of comfort, when the actual fault lies in the smallness of the sleeve, which will not allow it to " breathe ".

Another useful tip is this. *Never lose sight of the internals of your coat.* Many a costly alteration has been carried out (unhappily, with little or no effect) when the real cause of the trouble has been tight (or small) canvas and linings. This kind of fault is chiefly to be found in linings across the upper part of the back and the shoulders of the forepart. Have your canvas put in on the bias. It helps the tailor in his working out of the breast.

Now for a few hints about the *waistcoat*. It never does any harm to have *a little extra length of back*. This, in fact, helps to counteract the creases that are found when the wearer is seated, and also assists in reducing the length which frequently shows between the top button and the neck. The width of the back-neck should be on the generous side. In this way you will avoid those nasty little creases that are all too frequently to be seen in the shoulders.

Keep the waistcoat slightly *large on the top button*. This policy allows the waistcoat to fall better and prevents it from standing off at the lower buttons. Keep the waist cut and the bottom pockets low: you will find that by this means the general waist effect is improved.

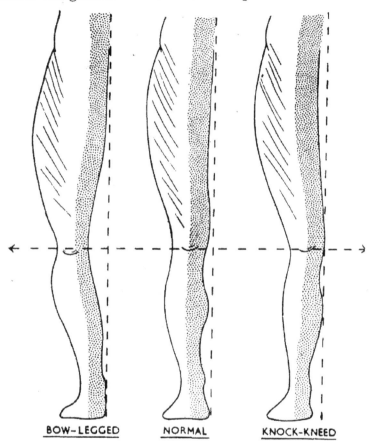

BOW-LEGGED   NORMAL   KNOCK-KNEED

FIG. 17.

The same principle applies to the trousers. *Keep them easy* in the original cutting. You will have fewer complaints, and certainly give yourself far less trouble, by erring on the big side.

Keep the *seat-line well back towards the side-seam.* You should not alter the angle unless you think it necessary.

Some of the better-fed bulks for which you have to cater will require almost elephantine amplitude into which to drop. Remember it is much easier to take in the fork than to let it out, particularly if the only inlay you can spare consists of selvedge.

In regard to the openness and closeness of legs, I advise you to steer a middle course. This I do because of the difficulty of altering the legs when once the trousers have been cut, and more so, of course, when they have been finished.

The knock-kneed and bow-legged fraternities present you with a bit of a problem. (Have a glance at Fig. 17.) Don't take me too literally when I tell you that in dealing with those whose knees scrape, I aim at *hitting them on the knee* and standing off slightly from the inside of the foot. With bandy legs I touch the knee at the outside and stand off slightly at the outside of the foot. In each cast I attempt to furnish the owners of the legs with an appearance of rectilinearity with which neither their parents nor, indeed, Mother Nature had quite succeeded in endowing them. In short, , the key-word is, closer for the former, and more open for the latter.

There is not much that I can add about the Minor Balances, but you will find that your safety-first pre-cautions are fairly self-evident.

CHAPTER X

SUITING STRANGE CUSTOMERS

Tom may be of normal build, Dick may be blessed with the fantastic proportions of a Falstaff, and as for Harry, you may think (quite privately, of course) that he is a wizened little worm. But if Tom, Dick and Harry happen to be your customers, it is your job to suit and satisfy them all. We have already touched on this matter; now let us go into it in a little more detail.

Our friend with *one shoulder low* is a downright nuisance. I mean this literally, for there are, of course, more low right than low left shoulders. Possibly the explanation is that most people are right-handed—I don't know. What we are up against here might well be called the fitters' problem child, or, better still, " problem children " —for they are triplets. By which I mean that there are at least three quite distinct varieties of dropped shoulder, each of which calls for a different diagnosis and a separate cure. These are:—

(1) The drop where the shoulder is thrown backwards, with a collapse of the ribs at the back of the arm.

(2) The vertical drop, with a collapse of the ribs under the arm.

(3) The drop with the shoulder thrown forward and a collapse of the ribs in front of the arm.

Generally speaking, all three are accompanied by a prominent hip on the offending side. Items (1) and (3) above are difficult to deal with. Item (2) is simple—so simple, in fact, that most cutters apply it to all three varieties, hoping for the best, but fearing (and, I regret to say, generally getting) the worst. Let us have a look at each.

Item (1): *Drop with shoulder back.* See Fig. 18. You

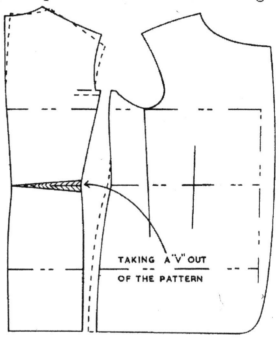

TAKING A "V" OUT
OF THE PATTERN

DROP—WITH SHOULDER
THROWN BACKWARDS
FIG. 18.

will discover that the effect will be a series of horseshoe folds, running from the blades towards the side-waist, whilst the offending side rests on the hip. The cause of this phenomenon is that the Minor Vertical Balance is too long, whilst the Minor Lateral Balance is too wide. Your Immediate Action must be to shorten the side-seam in relation to the back-seam. This you do by throwing the back-seam inwards at the top, lowering the neck-point and reducing the Minor Vertical Balance by the appropriate amount. Lower the top of the side-seam the same amount. Only the back section need be altered. You will adjust your Minor Lateral Balances by reducing the width of the back and letting out the hip on the forepart to the appropriate extent.

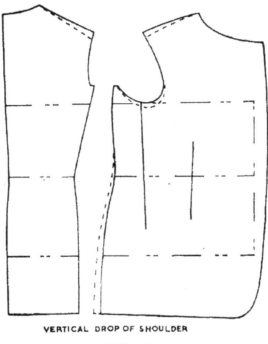

VERTICAL DROP OF SHOULDER

FIG. 19.

When putting the side-seam together, strain up the back slightly, so as to allow for the amount that the top of the back side-seam has been dropped. You can easily demonstrate for yourself the adjustment necessary by taking a " V " out of a pattern, ½ inch at the waist of the side-seam, to nothing at the centre back.

Item (2): *Vertical Shoulder Drop.* See Fig. 19. Here the effect reveals itself as a looseness at the shoulder-point, with lateral creases under the arm. The cause of this is, of course, that the shoulder is too square. Your Immediate Action will consist in reducing the Minor Vertical Balance in the same way as you would for a sloping shoulder, and in lowering the armhole the same amount.

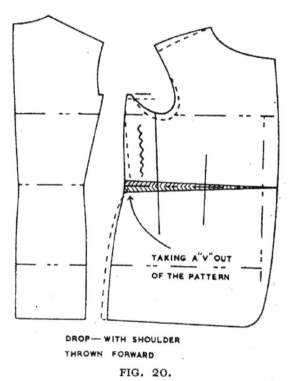

TAKING A "V" OUT

OF THE PATTERN

DROP— WITH SHOULDER

THROWN FORWARD

FIG. 20.

Item (3): *Drop with Shoulder Forward*. See Fig. 20. The effect consists of horseshoe folds in front of the arm, also from the neck-point towards the side-waist. You will notice an appearance of looseness across the front shoulder. Lastly, the collar will stand off on the offending side.

There are two causes to consider; they are:—

(*a*) The Minor Vertical Balance of the front is too long.

(*b*) The Minor Lateral Balance of the front is too wide.

To remedy these defects apply the following Immediate Action. First, adjust your vertical balance, reducing it by the appropriate amount through the front shoulder. Lower your armhole and also the top of the side-seam. Only the front section need be altered. Next you must adjust the lateral balances by narrowing the front of the shoulder, and at the same time letting out the hip. When you come to put the side-seam together, strain up the forepart of it to the extent that it has been dropped. You may demonstrate this action for yourself by taking a " V " out of the pattern $\frac{1}{2}$ inch at the waist, to nothing at the front edge.

Our next strange customer is the gentleman with prominent blades, sloping shoulders and a pigeon chest, all rolled into one. We meet with him not infrequently, and he is perhaps the most difficult customer, first to fit, and then to camouflage. He, of all the people we shall commonly meet, will provide our system with the acid test. And I am in the happy position to assure you that the method I have taught you emerges from this, its severest test, completely vindicated. I know, because I have proved it in practice.

This kind of figure almost invariably causes distress to the tyro cutter. He is prone to complain, " When I look at the back, which is standing off the body, I decide to pass up the back. But when I look at the forepart, which sticks out at the front, I decide upon a longer front balance. What the dickens am I supposed to do next? "

He certainly is in a dilemma, but obviously he can't have it both ways, and hence *he must leave the Major Vertical Balance alone* and seek the cause of the effects elsewhere.

E

Following the sequence of fitting, then, we look first to the Major Lateral Balance. This, we decide, is correct. Next we attend to our Minor Vertical Balances and make the necessary adjustments for sloping shoulders.

But we have still not found the real cause of our trouble, which consists of an *apparent* shortness of balance both back and front. So we turn to our final group (the Minor Lateral Balance adjustments), and at last we are rewarded by *discovering both causes*. In the back section we find that there is *insufficient blade-room*, causing the back to stand off, and also giving an appearance of short back balance. Across the chest we find that there is a *lack of chest-room in the right place* sufficient to cover the pigeon chest comfortably. We notice that here the cloth rests flatly on the chest, causing an appearance of short front balance by reason of the forepart standing off at the bottom.

The adjustment is simple in the back section, because we have a back-seam in which the necessary alteration for shape can be made by letting out over the blades. It is not, however, so simple in the front section, because there is, of course, no seam through the breast (as in a ladies' coat) to enable us to provide the shape in the right place.

So we are forced to provide one by means of a cut. Let the coat out, say, $\frac{1}{4}$ inch right through the front edge, taking the surplus material below the breast away (with a cut of a similar amount) from the bottom through the waist to nothing at the nipple. By this means we attain the shape necessary to allow the cloth to encompass the prominent parts of the figure comfortably, instead of merely resting upon them.

Thus we have had to plough all through our drill, right to the last sequence, before we succeeded in detecting the cause in this instance. Don't be downhearted by reason of that. Console yourself rather with the fact that *by employing a systematic sequence of tests to your fitting no fault can remain undetected.* You will eventually, by means of a persistent and methodical pursuit, track down the cause of any effect. Having found the cause, I am quite sure that by now you can apply the cure for yourself. And so you have, to that extent, become adept at suiting some strange customers.

CHAPTER XI

CARCASE AND CAMOUFLAGE

Up to the present we have concentrated for the most part upon the basic groundwork of your trade. Now let us turn for a short while to some of the fancy stuff. I am thinking at the moment of that much-sought-after and graceful garment known as the Draped Coat, of which it may truly be said that " distance lends enchantment to the view". In my humble opinion it does not bear inspection too closely, because it does not really fit. Rather, as the name applies, it drapes the figure, and if you are going to adopt this style to any great extent you must be prepared to educate your customers' tastes.

In spite of these remarks, I consider that the draped coat is to be commended, not only for its graceful lines, but also for its comfort, and its *ability to camouflage* the many and varied imperfections of the human figure. It so happens that it is the one and only garment our ready-made competitors find difficulty in producing. The reason for this is that cutting the coat doesn't finish the job. It is a tailored garment in the old-fashioned sense of the term, and so is easy to cut, but difficult to make.

The journeyman who aspires to make a draped coat must have a flair for his job, with more than a touch of artistry in his make-up. Such are few and far between to-day, but I believe that, caught young enough, the enthusiast can be taught all that is necessary in this regard.

I have said that the draped coat is easy to cut. The

cutter should possess, above all things, the quality of audacity. Don't be afraid of the job. Be bold; be daring. The chief characteristics of the coat are its size in the top section and the correspondingly small, egg-shaped armhole. It is shown to the most elegant advantage when worn by the tall man, with square shoulders. On the other hand, it serves its most *useful* purpose in cases where a misused waist has gained in superiority over the poor old chest.

A 40-inch chest with a 40-inch waist is seldom a thing of beauty. But if only we can contrive to convey the *appearance* of a 44-inch chest rising above the 40-inch waist, we are well on the way to earning the undying gratitude of the misshapen wretch who (in a moral moment) threatens himself with a sober diet of orange juice and steamed fish, but who (in the ultimate issue) out-gourmandizes most of his fellow-gourmands.

This is how it is done. Cut a wide back and a small forepart at the side seam. All your craft will be required in disposing of the extra width of back shoulder occasioned by the extra width of back. An inch, or even more, is not considered excessive. The fulling-on process has the effect of shortening the side in relation to the centre back, allowing the extra width to drape in a graceful fold from the end of the shoulder to the waist. Obviously, it is this *extra width across the back* that makes for comfort as well as elegance.

A similar drape must be imparted to the front of the armhole. This you obtain by advancing the *Major Lateral Balance*—that is, the neck-point—anything up to an inch, and letting out the front of the chest a similar amount. By this means, the drape, or extra chest room, is transferred to the front of the arm, resulting, in the hands of the craftsman, in a similar drape to that of the back from the shoulder-point, straight down towards the waist.

The observant student may well ask why, if it is necessary to full-on the back in order to hold up the width in that section, it is not also necessary to full-on the front shoulder to perform a similar function for the front section. The answer is, of course, that you *can't full-on both of them*. You must look for some other means of holding up the excessive width across the chest. How is this to be done?

You will remember that in a previous chapter we spoke of the " internals " of the coat. Here they are a most important factor. You must work out the centre of the breast to give a relative shortness to the front of the scye. This is the only method by which the extra width can be maintained in the place where we want it. The operation will fail unless the canvas is put in long and on the bias. The shoulder lining, too, should be long, so that it is able to render its assistance.

I must warn you of one difficulty that you are quite likely to experience with this type of coat. You may find that the drape *refuses to run straight up and down*, particularly if you have not had much experience of making this kind of shoulder. The drape at the top may show an awkward tendency to steal away at an angle, towards the middle of the shoulder. This fault is difficult to eradicate. What is the cause? It is simply that the inside is too small, and so prevents the cloth from going where it wants to go and where it is intended to be.

The shoulder should be made up soft, and not " nailed down " around the armhole. If your customer has a square figure, a small, stiffish pad in the shoulder-point is all the wadding you will require. But for a figure of the sloping kind be more generous with your padding, a greater amount of which will be needed to hold up the drape.

How are you going to cope with the modern Falstaff—

the corpulent *bon-vivant*, whose chest has slipped in the course of years well below his waist-line? The " bowler hat " is scarcely easy to conceal! I advise you not to worry unduly until you meet a waist that exceeds in size its neighbouring chest. When you do come across it, you must take it in hand.

The old-fashioned remedy was to throw a receptacle for the bowler (or belly) by taking out what was known as a belly cut (horrible phrase!). All this ever succeeded in doing, however, was to accentuate the wearer's natural ungainliness. The big cut from the back of the pocket-mouth through to the armhole had the effect of flattening the chest, and so giving the coat the appearance of the figure—in other words, making it look bottom heavy. If you are going to cheat the ravages of nature, your policy must be to aim in the reverse direction.

The shoulders must be draped—you know how to do that. A small waist-cut can be taken out in the usual way. The front of the coat will be found to be resting on the belly, at just about the front of the pocket. Keep that coat fairly generous across the waist, so that its resting-place is not too obvious. You will also find some surplus material standing off at the bottom, below the front of the pocket. This must be taken away by a cut (of the appropriate amount) exactly where it asks for it—from the bottom, through to the pocket-mouth. By keeping the coat slightly long in front you will help to preserve the general illusion.

I can assure you that once you have tickled the fancy of your most corpulent customer with a draped coat, he will have such an awed respect for it that never again will he carelessly fling it over the back of his chair as he turns his most earnest attention to the carving of the Sunday joint.

CHAPTER XII

BEST BIB AND TUCKER

In this short chapter I am going to give you a few hints on the making of body-fitting coats. At this stage it is scarcely necessary for me to say that you will apply to morning and to dress coats the same system of balance adjustment, in preparing the pattern and fitting, as you have done for the jacket of a lounge suit.

As the name implies, body-fitting coats cling more closely to the figure than the jacket, although it is nevertheless permissible to have a drape effect at the shoulder.

The designers of these garments have shown great consideration for the tailor (in assisting him to fit the body closely) by placing at his disposal two extra seams—namely, the back side-body (or round) seam and the waist-seam. The round seam is most useful, in that it provides shape to the back section. It could be used for an adjustment of the Major Vertical Balance if necessary, though it will rarely be called upon to serve that function in practice. Normally the operation will be carried out by the passing up or down of the side-body forepart seam. Thus you are safe in saying that our round seam is used for Minor Lateral adjustments only. By increasing the size at the blades, or by reducing it at the waist, the shape of the figure is found and the correct fitting is obtained.

Similarly, the waist (or skirt) seam gives us some assistance in providing shape to the front section. We can make adjustments of Minor Lateral Balance by means of cuts (or darts) taken out at the waist where they are needed.

In this way the shape of the chest is provided and the fitting of the waist is obtained.

In the fitting of the skirt adjustments of Minor Vertical Balance and of Minor Lateral Balance will be necessary. You must take the greatest care in determining the amounts of the required adjustments, as otherwise small, but unsightly, creases will appear in the vicinity of the waist-seam at the hips, and, in addition, the pleats may either overlap or open.

Your Minor Vertical adjustments are arrived at by means of a happy marriage of the waist of the skirt to the waist of the body. Here your system (or block) patterns will provide the basis for preparing the pattern, but you will have to watch it very carefully when fitting. The adjustment is a simple minor one, for the small, almost insignificant creases are just crying out to be relieved of their pain. It is strangely true, nevertheless, that many body-coats that in all other respects fit the wearer well are spoilt merely by the maladjustment of this minor balance.

The Minor Lateral adjustment merely concerns the size of the hips and the seat, and whether these be bigger or smaller than usual you must make proper provision for them. If you decide that it is necessary to place round on the pleat in order to cover a large seat, don't run it in *too abruptly* at the top. Take away the surplus by a cut in the skirt waist, in line with the side-body seam, and so provide a receptacle for the seat.

CHAPTER XIII

TALLY HO!

AGAIN, instead of the usual meal, I am going to treat you to a soupçon in this chapter. In dealing, very shortly, with jodhpurs and riding-breeches, I would first observe that the same principles apply to each of them.

So long as you are well acquainted with your "balance tables" you may set your mind at rest, because the designers of jodhpurs and riding-breeches have made the cutting a comparatively simple job. A seam is provided for you exactly where you want it, in order to supply a receptacle for the knee.

Before attending to the minor adjustments, however, we must employ a Major Lateral movement in opening the legs considerably, in order to conform to their position when their possessor is in the saddle.

The seam under the knee calls for an adjustment of the Minor Vertical Balance, the exact amount being dependent on the position of the legs when in the saddle, *in which position breeches should, of course, be fitted.* Be guarded, however, in your enthusiasm, so that you do not clear the underside so thoroughly as to render it impossible for the wearer to stand erectly when out of the saddle.

It may help to impress this last point upon your memory if I tell you about the dear old gentleman who, in the course of dressing one morning, complained that he could not raise his body to its normal position. His daughter, quite alarmed, hurriedly called in the doctor, who made a rapid appreciation of the situation, correctly diagnosed the trouble and prescribed an immediate action cure, to the great relief of all concerned. All he did was to release the bottom button-hole of the waistcoat, into which the poor old chap had inadvertently fastened a lower button of the fly of his trousers. You could describe the case as one of " front Minor Balance adjustment too short ".

CHAPTER XIV

ALMOST AN AFTERTHOUGHT

I FIND I have said nothing about overcoats. There is not, indeed, much that I can say now. So this chapter is another sartorial snack.

The making of overcoats is an interesting subject, and, to the person who already has a grip of the mechanics of cutting and fitting a jacket, not too difficult.

An overcoat is comparatively easy to fit, not only because of its generous lines, but also because the nature of the cloth used is such that the many minor ailments from which the under-garments might suffer in like circumstances will not be apparent.

Because of the simplicity in fitting, the big manufacturing tailors have largely filched this class of business from the bespoke tailor, although the discerning customer obviously still prefers the bespoke product. How long he will be able to continue doing so depends on how long our craft will be allowed to survive. Of that, however, more anon.

You will enjoy making overcoats because of the licence you are allowed, and because of the scope there is for original and imaginative thinking in the production of their varied styles. Your work embraces a wide field. At one end of the scale we have the fly-fronted Chesterfield demanded by the City gentlemen, and at the other the Harris tweed Inverness Cape, so much sought after by the kilted Highlander.

The full-hanging (or swinging) coat calls for an exact

adjustment of the Major Vertical Balance, in order to produce the flare just where it is wanted. You already know how to obtain the desired effect by passing the balance up or down, or by leaving it stationary.

There is one unsightly effect, frequently found in overcoats, which you must take care to avoid when fitting. I refer to the tendency to *kick off at the bottom of the forepart*, particularly when the customer is corpulent. What happens is that the cloth rests on the belly and stands away in an ugly fold at the bottom, in a similar manner to that explained in connection with jackets for the " bowler-hatted." A cut such as suggested there (from the front of the pocket through to the bottom) is quite effective, but it is rather inartistic in an overcoat. It follows, therefore, that your only alternative is to have recourse to the previously despised belly-cut through the pocket-mouth up to the armhole.

CHAPTER XV

LET'S JOIN THE LADIES

I HAVE been asked by a friend who has read these notes so far, why I have said nothing about cutting for ladies.

The short answer, of course, is that there is nothing much to say about it, for the simple reason that my new balance method of instruction applies equally and effectively to the cutting and fitting of any garment, whether it be for the male or female.

It is an interesting point, however, and might at least serve as a useful *minor* lesson.

Most ladies' cutters proceed in the same way as cutters for men. They prepare the pattern for the individual either by drafting from a well-tried system, or from an equally well-tried block pattern.

It follows, therefore, that the same balance adjustments will apply in preparing the pattern, and the same procedure or " drill " will be followed in the fitting-room, as those already explained.

The two major balances and the minor vertical balances will be arrived at in the same way, but the minor lateral balances (those, you will remember, being for shape and size) will be simplified by the fact that the placing of seams is not bound by such arbitrary laws as obtain in the cutting of men's coats.

You can, if you wish, put a seam more or less where you like—a great help in placing the shape and size exactly where it is being called for.

70

The back and front panel seams will illustrate what I mean, the former being of great assistance in finding the shape of the back, whilst the latter is of inestimable value in finding or providing the shape for the front.

To that extent it may be true to say that ladies' cutting is perhaps easier than cutting for men—a remark which I fear will bring forth showers of protests from those who are interested only in ladies' cutting.

There is a school, chiefly to be found among the Continental masters of ladies' cutting, who treat system in block production of patterns with complete and delightful contempt, whilst they proceed, " by rock of eye ", to rough out on canvas or linen the original crude production.

They rely solely on the " art of fitting " in balancing the various parts of the garment.

That they achieve success by this somewhat rule-of-thumb method cannot be denied, though it can be gained only at the expense of numerous and lengthy fittings, accompanied, I believe, by occasional swooning of the patient—the fitting becomes a kind of serial.

From the psychological angle there may be something to be said for this method, implying as it does that every garment is an original creation.

I prefer the system or block method of producing the pattern, and commend it to you.

There are certain characteristic features of female figures which have to be taken into account. It is not wise to lay down hard-and-fast rules about them; but here are one or two general observations.

They are, in most cases, flatter in the back section and fuller in the front than the male, calling for a shorter major vertical balance, to which no doubt your pattern-producing system, or block pattern—whichever you use—gives evidence.

Their figures in the main are rather easier to fit—not

being so muscular, they are perhaps more graceful. The shoulders are naturally squarer, which assists in giving effect to the draped coat.

Why ladies' tailors, having such delightful figures to work upon, distort them with grotesque shoulder-pads I cannot imagine, and why young women to whom nature has given such naturally artistic lines allow themselves to be paraded as a link between themselves and the anthropoid—I shall never know. Still, as they say in the North, " There is nowt so queer as folk ".

It is only fair to add that the better and more artistic ladies' cutters do not resort to this form of upholstery.

When the female becomes more matronly, and resorts to certain artificial devices to maintain her figure, she usually only succeeds in pulling herself in here, to push herself out there. This presents something of a problem to the novice. Let me therefore take you by the hand all through the labyrinth of major and minor balances once more and see what happens when preparing the pattern.

Major Vertical Balance

Our observations, when measuring, point to a fatty substance covering the blades, giving a thick or round back effect, which at first sight suggests a longer vertical back balance. Before making a decision on this important factor, we turn our attention to the observations and notes we have made of the front section, and find that the bust development suggests a longer front balance. The one cancels out the other; so we decide to keep to our block balance, which we have already seen is basically shorter than the male block.

Major Lateral Balance

This is the fore and aft of the forepart. Having decided, in order to obtain the shape of front, to cut a panel seam, there is no apparent reason to alter the neck-point, so the major lateral balance is left in accordance with the block pattern. We next turn our attention to the

MINOR VERTICAL BALANCES

Here we might find the shoulder normal from the neck-point to half-way along the shoulder-seam, with a definite falling away towards end of shoulder. This calls for minor vertical balance adjustment in the same way as you would do for the sloping shoulder; but, owing to the abrupt drop, and in the interest of the shoulder appearance, you will compromise by taking rather less than you would normally do, and make up by inserting a rather thicker shoulder pad.

Finally we come to the

MINOR LATERAL BALANCES

Here we find we have a tremendous lot to do. The heavy-looking, fat back in the vicinity of the blades falling away abruptly at the back arm calls for very careful minor lateral adjustments. To get the shape of the back in the right place, a panel seam over the blades is most useful in giving effect to your observations.

The hips and seat may be flat or prominent; your measures and observations will tell you where to increase or reduce the pattern local to requirements.

Turning to the front section, you must decide how much to increase or reduce your bust allowance from the normal. This can be readily done by giving the panel seam the appropriate shape—that, of course, being the shape of the figure.

Each minor lateral balance will have to be catered for in a similar way. Your measures and observations of the figure will tell where and how.

F

FITTING-ROOM SEQUENCE OR DRILL

Whilst fitting the jacket, throw your mind back to the departures you made from the block when preparing the pattern, so that you know exactly from where you started.

MAJOR VERTICAL BALANCE

Although the balance was not altered from the normal, we might find the coat standing away from the back, pointing to a short back balance, but before coming to a decision, take a look at the front section. This we might find resting on the bust and standing away from the front, suggesting a short front balance.

So we leave it for a moment and look for the cause elsewhere.

MAJOR LATERAL BALANCE

This appears to be correct, so proceed to the next in sequence.

MINOR VERTICAL BALANCES

These, as you are well aware, vary with the shape of the figure, square or sloping shoulders, long or short neck.

In this case we have noted, in preparing the pattern, how the shoulder falls abruptly away at the arm end.

To fit the shoulder exactly would be inelegant, so we attempt—in the interests of appearance—to make the shoulder of the figure fit the coat, adjusting the minor balances with the aid of the tailor and a little extra padding: a very low stand to the collar might be indicated, and so to our final group.

MINOR LATERAL BALANCES

Here you will find most of your trouble, with many adjustments to make. To begin with, you will find the cause of the anomaly: an apparent shortness of balance both back and front. In the first place, insufficient width has been given in the top back section to cover comfortably the thick or fatty back in the vicinity of the blades, causing the coat to stand off at the bottom.

Turning our attention to the front section, we find that insufficient allowance has been made to encompass comfortably the bust, causing the coat to rest there, and stand off at the bottom front. More width is needed in both sections at the appropriate spots, to allow the coat to fall into its correct place.

The panel seams back and front are most useful in giving effect to these minor lateral balances.

I can almost hear you say, " I seem to have heard all this before." Well, of course you have. Most of it is to be found in pages 57 and 58 of this little book under the heading, " Our next strange customer ". At the same time, you might refer back to paragraph two of the present chapter.

The repetition will do no harm, as this is perhaps the most difficult figure, either male or female, that you will be called upon to fit.

All these tedious little balances must be pursued methodically and relentlessly, first in preparing the pattern and then, more relentlessly, in the fitting-room.

Go through them carefully one by one, and you will find that they will all marry or balance up in the end.

This is the last chance you will get before the alterations begin to cost you and your employer time and money.

Getting it right now and getting it right after repeated alteration is the difference between the artist and the artisan.

Taking coats to pieces after they have been forward-baisted or finished depresses your journeyman tailor, who is usually of a sensitive nature. He has great respect for a cutter who knows his job, but an equal contempt for the butcher.

Every minor balance, whether it be vertical or lateral, must be correct before you can achieve success. Practise the method of procedure assiduously, both in preparing the pattern and in the fitting-room.

In time you will develop a selective instinct or flair: you will know at once whether it is better, in the general interest of the garment, to take in here or let out there to gain the same local effect.

A flair is something that can be cultivated: you need not necessarily be born with it. The way to cultivate it in the art of cutting and fitting is to learn the basic principles of balance and then to exercise unceasingly your powers of observation.

It will take time and infinite patience, but if it is true that " genius is the art of taking pains ", then you are well on its track; so don't despair.

> " It's not so difficult as that.
>   Just a game of tit for tat.
>   Bits off here or bits on there.
>   Observe and cultivate a flair."

Finally I would recommend all young ladies' cutters to take a course of training in rough sketching.

A lady when choosing a style likes something original. A rough sketch quickly drawn in her presence will contribute in no small measure to the confidence she will have in your ability.

CHAPTER XVI

PADOLOGY

THE art of shoulder padding or shoulder formation is one which appears to have been sadly neglected among the tailors of this country. In others, notably the U.S.A., it seems to have received the attention it deserves.

Most of us have applied the rule-of-thumb method to this important part of our trade, leaving it to the journeyman tailor to fashion his pad, who, without knowing the shape of the shoulder he is asked to cater for, goes merrily on making up the same pad of two or more plies of wadding regardless of whether the shoulder is normal-square or sloping.

It is not only unscientific but also unintelligent to shape the cloth shoulder of a coat with little or no regard to the amount of building it is to receive either in width or thickness.

Some bespoke tailors I have observed use a cheaply made up pad of layers of wadding rudely stitched together by a plonking machine, resembling a poultice rather than a shoulder shape. Whilst others use countless layers of wadding baisted together until the pad looks (and feels) like a bed. One such was recently brought in to me for alteration. The customer complained that he was worn out by shoulder weight, even before he got to his office in the morning. No wonder, for, when taken out, the pad was found to consist of no less than thirty plies of wadding. And this was a West End production!

Other bespoke tailors use pads made up not of wadding,

but of harder or firmer substances, until the shoulder has got beyond even upholstery and encroached upon the art or craft of saddlery.

The cutter who is responsible for shaping the cloth to fit a shoulder is obviously the person to decide how much or how little padding should be inserted.

This is extremely difficult to achieve if it is left to the tailor to make up. Each individual has his own ideas on the subject, whilst the varying thicknesses and quality of wadding play an irregular part. It follows, therefore, that some sort of made-up pad is the solution to the problem.

The manufacturing clothier uses a made-up shoulder pad the width and thickness of which is carefully considered. It is subjected, I believe, to very severe tests— even to treatment by the Hoffman press before being put in; this, presumably, to enable the pattern designer to arrive at the overall allowance in the circumference of the armhole to take the pad comfortably.

The bespoke cutter will in time, I believe, have to adopt the made-up pad in the interests of efficiency. Gone are the days when alteration tailors were waiting upon you to take away or add another ply or two.

Sub-division, which I presume we must *all* come to in the not-far-distant future, calls for the made-up or fashioned pad. Many bespoke cutters will tell you their tailors object to using them. In other words, the tail wags the dog. Tailors must be instructed in their use and told of their advantages.

The type of shoulder pad used by the bespoke tailor should be one which is adaptable to the various shapes and sizes of shoulders and which at the same time eliminates, as far as possible, all evidence of padding.

It must be flexible or made up in the same way as the inside of the coat, the canvas and felt parts cut on the bias, so that it can be stretched if necessary to the formation of the canvas of the coat. The stubborn, unwieldy or firmly made set pad, whilst it may satisfy the cheaper or lower methods of tailoring, is of no use to the high-class bespoke tailor, whose object must always be to shape and mould the shoulder in an artistic manner, irrespective of the natural, and perhaps ungainly, shape of the wearer. He will be assisted in this respect by the use of a pad which I recently invented, and which I venture to bring to the notice of readers of this book.

It is designed not only to pad, but initially to *create* a shoulder line. Its canvas base extends from the neck point to the shoulder end. Its extended anchorage to the neck point helps to eradicate those tiresome little bumps and creases which are prone to appear when the pad finishes mid-shoulder. At the shoulder end an envelope is formed by felt attached to the canvas, into which the appropriate size pad is inserted, dependent on shape and size of shoulder. Its design renders it flexible, extendable and adaptable to any size or shape of shoulder.

For example, for the very square figure or for the modern cult of " no padding ", the frame only need be used. To this the sleeve-head wadding can be attached, thus giving a smooth and uninterrupted line to the shoulder. Another advantage of the adaptable pad is that it facilitates minor adjustments to the finished garment and is a great time-saver in this respect. When serging the armhole, the sleeve seam may be serged to the canvas part of the frame only, leaving the envelope open for simple pad adjustment, without having to take the whole shoulder to pieces; also a tail-piece of felt at forearm and hindarm is left on, enabling the tailor to attach a small soft pad to the former, in case of a hollow or falling away below a bony and forward shoulder, or, in the case of a full-busted lady's coat, a similar pad could be attached where the blades or the figure are carried very high, causing a " poorness " or falling-away at the back shoulder. Little touches of artistry such as these are part of a cutter's job and not that of the tailor.

This invention, simple as it is, may not be the last word in bespoke shoulder pads, but it is a very good start and I commend its use.

The pad is now being extremely well manufactured by Jaykay Shoulder Pads Ltd., Crabtree Hall, Crabtree Lane, London, S.W.6, from whom an explanatory leaflet may be obtained.

CHAPTER XVII

THE CUSTOMER IS ALWAYS RIGHT

OF course he is—on the surface. At the same time, you have your job to do, and he must not be allowed to interfere with your working efficiency. Never let him teach you your business. In order to help you to deal with awkward customers, I am going to end this little book on a lighter note, by putting you wise to a few of the whims and wiles of customers that you are likely to meet.

But first let me repeat the story told by an eminent General about another eminent British officer (no names no pack drill) who had recently been given a very important post in the Eastern theatre of war.

Before proceeding he called up a pre-eminent American General who had for some time held a similar appointment in the Western theatre, seeking perhaps a little advice, and was told, " There are two essentials to success ": (*a*) A first-class Chief of Staff; (*b*) a first-class tailor.

The advice was strictly followed, with the result that the eminent officer himself became pre-eminent.

How great a part the second portion of this advice played in his success we cannot say. But we craftsmen insist on taking a little credit.

I tell you this so that you may have a quiet conceit and pride in the importance of your calling—but don't wear the mantle until you deserve it.

In the fitting-room always be courteous, but *firm*. Sooner or later you will come across young *Mr. Nobby*

Knowall, who not only wants to order a suit, but also to tell you how to make it. Listen patiently to all he has to say, and then tell him politely, but with resolution, that you are prepared to consider suggestions he may make in regard to style, but that the fitting must be left entirely to you.

Then there is the *Hon. Cecil Sidetrack*, who invariably draws a red herring or two across your path by telling you the (alleged) latest funny story whilst you are fitting him. Let him, too, see (politely but surely) that at the moment you are more interested in fitting than in his humour. There is a time and place for everything and, anyhow, you had probably forgotten his particular anecdotes before you were out of the cradle.

Have you yet met that old teaser, *Mr. Philip Fidget?* He's a menace. He saws the air, lashing out with his arms like the sales of a windmill. He has ants in his pants. Pause to allow him to finish his physical jerks, and then (quietly, but not without determination) place his arms in their normal position and carry on. You will usually find that he is also a windbag, and that his next puff will set the arms in motion again. A quick step backwards (implying that you regard him as dangerous) may have a soothing effect. But carry on, gentling his restive limbs into position, and you will eventually wear him down. The keynote for success in dealing with him is, attrition—non-belligerent, of course.

Another customer you will meet is *Sir Pall Wearybore.* Having put the inmates of his club to sleep with his tedious talk, he'll slip round to see you. You will discover that much of your cutting time during the day can be wasted by allowing yourself to be buttonholed and forced to listen to his irrelevancies. A simple but effective way out of the difficulty is to have a pre-arranged plan with a junior, who is to enter and announce that Mr. So-and-

So awaits you in another fitting-room when you are free.

The wife of poor little *Henry Henpeck*, like most female critics of men's clothes, can be vastly irritating, and she should be excluded from the fitting-room whenever possible. Rarely is her criticism helpful: frequently it is ridiculous. *Never, on any account, allow her in until the fitting is concluded.* If then this virago proves troublesome, you are in a position to escape and send a junior in to pick up the pieces.

I once lost a good customer by allowing his wife into the fitting-room. There may have been others, but I remember this one in particular. She complained that the fly of her husband's trousers, instead of disappearing amidships at the bottom, took a cant to the right. I pointed out that there was a physical reason for the phenomenon, which I could not explain in her presence. The husband expressed himself as satisfied with my explanation, but I never saw him again. I wonder, did he die a martyr to his wife's æsthetic tastes?

Another story—also a true one—concerns a sartorially wife-ridden customer who worked out his salvation in his own way. Accompanied by his wife, he entered an establishment, saying to the salesman, " I want a *brown* suit." His wife immediately countered with, " *No*, you are going to have a *blue* suit." The husband submitted, with apparent good grace, and a blue suit was selected. When his wife was out of earshot, he slyly explained that that was the colour he had intended to have from the start.

I tell you these stories not merely to pass the time of day, but because they hold a lesson for you. If only you can adjust yourself mentally, a sense of good humour will help you in many an awkward situation. I know it is difficult to see the brighter side when you are doing your best to please *Mr. Ivor Grouse* in one fitting-room whilst from the next room you can overhear *Colonel Peevish Crabbe* fuming as he awaits attention from you. But a smile will take the old war-horse off his guard, and the major complaint will have developed into a minor one even before you begin.

Take heart. The fitting-room (like some of the ideologies and like poverty, too) is a great leveller. The most bombastic customer seems but insignificant when you have got him with his pants down. They say that no man is a hero in the eyes of his valet. The same is true as between a customer and his tailor, to whom many of his foibles and petty conceits are exposed.

For a comfortable and easy-going life give me the Provinces. The provincials, bless 'em, are easier to please and less clothes-conscious than your West End customer. Further, you will find far fewer bad debts amongst them. These are only some of the recommendations to a life out of London.

In business, you will find John, Taffy, Jock and Paddy easier to please than Pierre, Hans, Antonio or Fritz. Jock, too, is the best payer of all. Probably the reason why the Britisher is the best-dressed man in the world is that he doesn't fuss—he is content to go to a first-class tailor and trust him to see the job through. Your foreigner, on the other hand, usually regards the whole world with a distrustful eye. Perhaps he has been caught too often in his own country. However, in the main you will find that the Continentals are fairly easy to handle: most of them are cast in the same mould, and knowing one, you know the lot. Match their aggression and self-assertiveness with your own. In this way you will get them where you want them. Many of them fall for sales talk more readily than the Britisher, who is not so easily kidded. With the latter you must do your stuff by subtle implication, by talking of artistry and craftsmanship, and by insinuating that clothes can be made to enhance individual personality. How different from the States, where height and rotundity are a man's sole distinguishing characteristics so far as his clothes are concerned.

The Englishman frequently repays your insinuative tactics in kind, particularly in these days of supply shortage, if he suspects you're a bit slow in delivering the goods. Now, your foreigner (within a week or so of placing his order) will employ the lie direct. He will bounce in, announcing (quite naïvely) that he was just passing the door and has called to see if by any chance you were ready for a fitting.

By contrast, Paddy (from the Emerald Isle) will, in all probability, forget that he ever placed an order, and on receipt of a postcard telling him that his fitting is ready, he will ring up to say that he has used up his overdraft for something else, and " Wh-hat would I be doin' about that now, Mister?"

Jock, of course, will call in to fill his fountain pen, and, incidentally, write a small, but welcome, cheque on account—perhaps so as to soften the blow to himself when the bill arrives.

But the Englishman (God bless him!) has got them all whacked. Dropping in, he is wont to waffle. " Being in the vicinity, old boy, and the hour being that of opening time, I wondered whether, old boy, you'd care to join me and blow the froth off one." There's insinuation for you! Most of us fall an easy victim to his devices. On departing he may go so far as to remark casually, " Well, cheerio, old man. See you soon." To which you meekly retort, " Very well, sir. I'll be ready for you on Monday." And so from start to finish he has not uttered one word touching his real purpose, but in his charming way he has attained his end.

I am afraid that in this, our final association together, I've been a trifle discursive. But I will wind up now by reiterating that few men are endowed with figures that can be *fitted* and remain good to look upon. Clothes, therefore, should be emblematic.

It saddens me that even on demobilisation the Powers that Be regimented our Service men once more to the extent of doling them all out with a suit cut from the same block, so creating the appearance of a robot army in civilian dress. Perhaps that was inevitable. But such a proceeding tends to cause uniformity of habit in clothes.

We must face the fact that our craft is in *danger of extinction*. It is the oldest and will, I believe, be the last to go, as one by one they are ruthlessly destroyed at the guillotine of the industrialist, the politician and the scientist, all of whom appear to take a sadistic delight in seeing such majestic but melancholy heads rolling in the dust. Can we survive? Assuredly, yes. But we shall do so only so far as we succeed in invigorating the trade with more recruits as craftsmen. Where could we better seek than amongst our own sons and daughters, whose roots are already there? Unbounded possibilities are theirs in an interesting, not overworked, yet a well-paid career.

INDEX

PRINTED IN GREAT BRITAIN BY THE EDEN PRESS
(R. J. SKINNER LTD.)
4 CARMELITE STREET, LONDON, E.C.4.